BARRY LOFTON

MASTER YOUR FOCUS

The Ultimate Guide The Power of Focus, Discover The Secrets on How You Can Improve and Master Your Focus In Order to Unlock Your Inner Greatness

Descrierea CIP a Bibliotecii Naţionale a României
BARRY LOFTON
  MASTER YOUR FOCUS. The Ultimate Guide The Power
of Focus, Discover The Secrets on How You Can Improve and
Master Your Focus In Order to Unlock Your Inner Greatness /
Barry Lofton. – Bucharest: Editura My Ebook, 2020
  ISBN

BARRY LOFTON

MASTER YOUR FOCUS

The Ultimate Guide The Power of Focus, Discover The Secrets on How You Can Improve and Master Your Focus In Order to Unlock Your Inner Greatness

My Ebook Publishing House
Bucharest, 2020

TABLE OF CONTENTS

CHAPTER 1

"FOCUS" DEFINED

Focus is integral to accomplishment. It may actually fall in the same category as ambition, motivation, leadership and other driving forces behind becoming successful, but does not necessarily get the attention that it deserves. Often downplayed, the role of focus cannot be sabotaged in an individual's ability to be productive.

What all this basically means is that you need to be focused in order to achieve something or become successful in your endeavors. But before we go into that, here is a look at what focus really means.

By definition, focus is a skill that allows people to start a task without procrastination and then keep up their attention and effort until the job is complete. It is an ability to not only pay attention to things that they are engaged in but also avoid distractions that will impede the work they are trying to do.

In fact, focus is so important to getting anything done that you can't really think without focus. When you hear about things like perception, memory, learning, reasoning, decision making and problem solving, you know that none of these can be done successfully unless you focus.

On the contrary, a wandering mind will make you less effective in your work and your productivity will suffer. The same will also compromise the quality of work giving you less than optimal results. Not to forget that you will also be wasting time every instance your mind drifts off.

Why do people suffer from a lack of focus?

In some cases, a lack of focus may be a matter of interest. Take your everyday to-do list for instance. Not everything on the list might be interesting to work on, but needs to get done anyways for you to move ahead. In these instances you may find yourself stuck, trapped doing something that you couldn't care less about. Your only obligation may be the feeling that you need to get the job done to move on to other things. Not such a great motivator, but that's reality; in the real world things need to get done to make way for other things.

It is only natural that your mind starts to drift off in these situations. You may end up finding excuses for not doing that particular thing, say by justifying that you don't really *need* to do the job right then, or that it's not really *that* important or even something like you've got *better things* to do than the job on hand. But any way you dress them up, they are all just excuses for procrastination.

Which brings us to another aspect of focus; procrastination. Procrastination is perhaps the biggest hurdle in the way of attaining good focus. When you use procrastination to get out of things what you are really saying is that you don't want to do a particular task, or that you are secretly hoping that it will just go away on its own, or that you will *eventually* feel motivated to do it.

With so much going on, it is no wonder that focus gets sidelined and never surfaces to the forefront.

And while a lot more can be said on procrastination, we will cross that bridge when we come to it (in a later chapter). For now, it is sufficient to say that procrastination, in fact, is the granddaddy of all excuses and will never let you focus properly on any given task.

How can you counter a lack of focus?

Moving on, while you may be well aware of what is stopping you from focusing (think procrastination), you may not know how to tackle this problem. So here's some help:

- **Address WHAT needs to be done**

To make focus work for you, you need to have a **clear cut goal**; call it a grounded purpose towards which all your efforts are directed. When you have this reference point in sight, you can apply all your skillset and decision making to get the job done right. But with this crucial factor missing, you may as well go on a roller coaster ride.

It is these clear cut goals that define what needs to get done.

Clear cut goals also stop you from derailing and prevent you from going places where you never intended to go. Pick out a typical day in your life and think of all the fifty or so things you need to do. With your mind divided and scattered trying to deal with all fifty at the same time, you are likely not going to get much done. On the flip side, you may actually neglect to do some of the more important ones as you keep thinking about everything else instead.

This is a point where focus can come save your day. Using focus, work by the process of elimination and prioritize your goals. When you learn to prioritize your goals, you end up spending your time in a more meaningful way; the important stuff gets done first and the not-so-important later on.

Filtering out such time-eaters also help you regain control over chaos and you no longer feel that you are wasting time.

- **Address WHY something needs to be done**

When clear cut goals are paired with a **sense of purpose** the dilemma starts to resolve itself fairly easily. This sense of purpose also verifies why something needs to be done.

People are naturally more motivated when they have a reason to do something. With that reason in mind, you will feel more inclined to perform better so you can get the results you seek. A sense of purpose will also fine tune your focus as you want to get the best results out of your efforts.

- **Also address WHEN something needs to be done**

This one ties in with prioritizing your goals so that important things get done first. Knowing when to do what can make everyday living so much easier to cope with.

Plus, giving yourself a timeframe to work within helps you stay on task i.e. stay focused so you can then have more time to do the other things you need to do.

Successful time management lets you take control of your life rather than follow others. Plus, you end up accomplishing more, performing better and becoming more successful at what you do. Added perks include a sense of satisfaction and peace of mind.

But whether it is prioritizing goals, finding a sense of purpose or practicing time management skills, none of it can be achieved without good focus.

Types of focus

Having established that the ability to focus is a critical element for success in aspect of life, let us now take a look at the different types of focus you need to develop to achieve that success.

Inner focus

This is the most common of all types. Inner focus is an individual's ability to block our distractions, focus on the present moment and task and stay calm under the pressure. This type of focus develops a person's intuition, gut feeling and good decision making.

The benefit of establishing inner focus allows to stay focused in your goals and manage your own schedule.

Focusing on others

Not everyone masters this type of focus as it goes beyond what you are doing and demands that you attend to what others are doing and saying instead. This type of focus is especially important in workplace situations or teamwork scenarios where your output is affected by others' input. However, this type of focus is not only restricted to professional settings, but is equally applicable to personal and social contexts as well.

Outer focus

Outer focus goes beyond paying attention to other people and demands paying attention to your surroundings instead. Outer focus is based on peripheral learning and allows a person to think strategically. It also allows for making adjustments to outer surroundings as circumstances around you change.

CHAPTER 2

ESCAPING THE BUSY TRAP

Being overwhelmed results in burnout. This produces a condition where the individual feels mentally, emotionally and physically exhausted. The feeling occurs when you feel overwhelmed and aren't able to keep up with demands. As a result chaos also factors into the equation and the missing element once again is focus.

The feeling of being persistently overwhelmed can easily cause you to lose interest as well as motivation and bring on a state that leaves you feeling powerless, helpless and extremely worn out. Once again, you may be trying to do too much- much more than it is realistic to handle.

When talking about burnout, remember that it is not mere exhaustion that you experience. It does not merely affect your performance but every aspect of life. For instance, work may become unbearable, but you will also lose interest in almost everything else that you do. Fun stops being fun while every insignificant thing starts to bother you.

In a state of burnout, this feeling does not go away but sticks around on a regular basis. In fact, staying in this forlorn condition will likely make you believe that there is no alternative or getting out of this mess.

So how do you get yourself out of this rut? You turn your attention to focus.

Remember what being focused taught you in the previous chapter? The WHAT, WHY and WHEN formula will come in very handy when you feel overwhelmed. Sort out issues by focusing on what's important, figure out why it is so and when to deal with it. Once you have the answers to these simple questions you can at least start to untangle the web of feeling overwhelmed.

Unraveling burnout

However, the problem with feeling overwhelmed is that it is not always possible to identify the burnout yourself. Experts recommend that when feeling distressed, seek out help from friends, family and others that you trust. They can not only give you an outside opinion but may also be able to help you out by citing examples of why they believe you may be burnt out.

Focus to undo the effects of the burnout

Once you have identified the trigger for your woes, be prepared to make some serious changes. This effort will take a lot of focus on your part as you will not only have to make serious changes but also stick with them for a while. The bright side to this entire episode is that once you start making the shift, you should also start to feel more motivated again. A good place to start is by focusing and working on some of the following:

- **Cut off the source of the burnout-** Where possible, shun the trigger that is causing you to feel overwhelmed. Job related burnouts often happen from too many hours working and too little personal time.

- **Try to be healthy-** Being overwhelmed can easily take a toll on health, so engage in some form of physical activity to give yourself a break. While taking a break may sound counterintuitive to focusing, the idea is to shift the focus from the cause of the burnout and redirect focus on taking care of yourself instead.

- **Eat well-** Focus on taking care of yourself by eating a little better than before. Chances are that being in a burnt-out state, you also neglected your diet. After all, the first thing most people reach for when overwhelmed is an abundance of junk and convenience foods. Chuck these out and refocus on what will make you feel better both on the inside and out.

- **Sleep better-** Last, but not least a burnout will bring forth long term exhaustion with it. The simple coping mechanism for this issue is to focus on getting both good quality and quantity of sleep.

When you want to get out of this despondent state, remember that focus is the one thing holding everything together. It is this ability to concentrate on your wellbeing that will allow you to remove all the negativity out of your life.

The impact of being overwhelmed

While you are in an internal state of being unfocused, things can go horribly wrong in the external world. Personal turbulence aside, the world keeps moving at its pace, continuing to bombard you with the daily grind, moving at a breakneck speed. With decisions and information piling up all the time, it becomes really hard to stay focused. And while you may not be able to detect so yourself, there are certain red flags that can identify the most common habits of unfocused people:

- **They don't plan**

It is very difficult to stay focused without a plan to execute. Unfocused individuals tend to work by whim, rather than by strategy. They seem to get into things that they "think" might be important without really knowing why. On the contrary, people who focus on their goals have a strategy to execute and move progressively through their agenda rather than randomly.

- **They lose track of time**

If you find yourself running short of time on most of your tasks, you are probably not focusing on good time management. You may be getting too deep into things, where it is not required and end up spending too much time on one specific task which, with focus and planning could have been allotted to multiple tasks instead.

Being unfocused also makes the individual struggle with keeping track of time.

- **They run late**

Closely tying in with poor time management is the susceptibility of always running late. Unfocused people not only tend to mismanage time but also exhibit unrealistic ideas about time.

For instance, a common tendency is to have an unclear idea about how long it takes to get to places. It becomes norm with such people to miscalculate distances or neglect outside factors that may affect travel times.

Another common scenario of being unfocused is when someone takes on a new project without finishing a previous one. The result is nothing but chaos where not many of the projects get done and the individual is left scampering to finish up while running behind on various tasks.

- **They get easily distracted**

People without focus are the easiest targets of distractions. That is to say that distractions are everywhere; some of them obvious, others not so much, but they do get in the way of getting things done.

If you are not focused, then every time you switch or shift from one activity to the next, there is a time lag in between. For unfocused folks, this void can easily be filled by sneaky distractions like getting on their cell phone, playing candy crush, and even a simple conversation is enough to take them far away from their assigned task. Does that sound like something that happens to you a lot? If so, you need to work on your focus.

- **They are messy, unorganized and possibly even flaky**

Being out of focus leaves its mark on the organizational skills of any person. Such people tend to be surrounded by clutter, unable to ever find what they are looking for and suffer gravely when it comes to productivity.

They are also unable to follow through on promises, tend to skip out on appointments and are quite prone to canceling at the last minute.

Unfocused people have a hard time committing and appear as flaky when they continuously fail to follow through. This not only harms their efforts but can be disastrous for their reputation.

- **They worry about everything**

If you find that you worry too much or get agitated over every small thing, you need to redirect your focus and channel it on things that are truly important. Learn to distinguish the substantial stuff from the insubstantial and then focus on that alone.

CHAPTER 3

RECLAIMING YOUR TIME

Now that you know that distraction is the main reason we lose focus, let us talk a bit about the various forms distractions can take. In many cases, these distractions may not seem as obvious as one imagines but may make you feel scattered or fuzzy instead. The result is that you may end up blaming yourself for not having more control.

At this point it is important to remember that as we get older, both focus and concentration can change, just as so can memory and other cognitive functions. However, this does not have to be inevitable. On the contrary, certain studies with older individuals reveal that the capacity for strategic learning or decision making may even improve with age.

There are certain habits and situations that can factor into impairing focus. Most are everyday habits that that be changed with some effort and may become the starting point for you to move ahead with gaining better focus and concentration.

Poor diet and nutrition

Food has a direct impact on cognition which is why a poor decision at lunch can derail an entire afternoon. Why this happens is because everything we eat is converted by the body into glucose providing energy. But not every type of food is processed by the body at the same rate.

So a poor diet that leads to hunger and dehydration can become a major distraction. Hunger can have a myriad of negative effects on health and behavior including the ability to focus. It is often tied in to low blood sugar that directly leads to fatigue and low energy levels.

Dehydration, on the other hand can lead to numerous symptoms that can reduce focus including headaches, fatigue and low mood. Studies establish that even 1% lower than optimal hydration can bring about a lack of focus.

So what are some of the pitfalls you need to avoid to let hunger and dehydration from setting in? Here's a look:

- **Weight loss diets**

Weight loss diets are notoriously bad for focus and concentration. Among these low fat diets can be held accountable as the brain needs essential fatty acids for proper functioning and these fats deprive the body of such nutrients. At the same time, cutting out on important nutrients like proteins is bad as well. This is because the amino acids in protein are essential for optimal brain performance in creating brain chemicals that improve focus.

- **Processed foods**

Poor nutrition, often in the form of empty calories does not give you the energy that you need. With insufficient energy, the brain has a hard time functioning or focusing on anything properly. As a result you may find that you experience mild irritability when you eat processed foods.

An example; eating processed foods such as cured meats can make the brain foggy. When you consume salt and protein rich foods like these there is a tendency to become dehydrated, and dehydration can diminish cognitive function.

- **Junk foods**

Junk foods are a whole different story by itself. Junk foods come in a high-fat, high-sugar and high-calorie package that gets digested fairly quickly. And while you may get instant gratification from eating these foods, they really don't do much to satisfy hunger.

Instead, since junk foods are devoid of nutrients, the body gets forced to engage sugar as a source of energy. This form of energy is quickly spent given the refined nature of sugar, leaving you with a sugar high also experienced as a temporary sensation of energy.

But after the metabolism has used up all the available energy, the surge is followed by a sugar crash accompanied by a feeling of fatigue, lethargy, focus loss and a wandering brain.

Hormones at play

Maintaining hormonal equilibrium is key to optimal brain functioning. It may surprise you to know that a deficiency of specific hormones can bring about significant changes in mental focus and processing.

With hormones out of whack you may find yourself having difficulty remembering people's names, snapping unintentionally, suffering from mood swings or even start to feel depressed. All these and other factors play a part in affecting the way your brain functions.

For women, the one thing to watch out for is estrogen levels. This female hormone can dictate everything from sugar cravings and bouts of fatigue to mood swings. Any imbalance is then seen as impacting mental agility where low estrogen levels can impair mental functions like memory, reasoning and even mood from running smoothly.

As a result women may often observe that fluctuations in estrogen levels during perimenopause and menopause may make their memory and attention wax and wane.

Another consideration that falls under hormonal imbalances and one that can impact the ability to focus is hypothyroidism. Low thyroid issues have been directly linked with causing mental fog, concentration issues, depression and even short term memory loss.

It is important that an optimal balance of estrogen, progesterone and testosterone is maintained since all three hormones act directly on nerve cells in the brain. Collectively, these hormones can help facilitate neurotransmission, protect cells from neurotoxins and improve blood flow in the brain. Any imbalance and the result could be a significant drop in cognition, mental focus and the ability to sustain concentration.

Lack of sleep

This common issue does not get the true attention it deserves. Even with a single night of insufficient sleep, the mind suffers greatly and focus becomes compromised. When you don't sleep well, your thought processes slow down and you become less alert. This affects your ability to concentrate and can make the mind confused enough to prevent you from performing tasks that require complex thought.

Also, feeling sleepy can cut into your working memory which is an important component of focusing. The sensation makes you less vigilant and reduces the speed and accuracy of mental tasks.

Stress

While memory and cognitive functioning gradually diminish with age, people with persistent or higher levels of stress are especially vulnerable. The negative effects of stress on memory can cause the brain to freeze and completely lose track of focus. This can happen in any scenario from students studying for an exam to introducing a friend and forgetting their name mid-way through introductions.

Focus caves in to stress in these situations as thinking gets so preoccupied with stress-inducing stimuli that other thoughts fail to emerge. In this way it hampers working memory which is associated with short term memory.

Lack of physical activity

Regular exercise releases brain chemicals which are key for memory and a lack of the same can impact focus and concentration. Exercise stimulates areas of the brain which are involved in memory functions. Physical activity releases a chemical called BDNF or brain derived neuro trophic factor which rewires memory circuits so they work better.

As such 30 minutes of exercise can help make more BNDF. But doing so once a week won't help. Exercise needs to be made a regular part of daily routine to reap cognitive benefits.

Surrounding environment

The environment where you are sitting down can quickly become a distracting factor when you are trying to concentrate. There could be multiple diversions such as loud noises, bright lighting, visual disruptions and even temperature inconsistencies.

Even though they may seem trivial, these environmental variables can play an important role in making or breaking focus.

Quality of information

Another common distraction is the quality of information you need to process. If the information is relevant to the task at hand, then it will likely keep your focus engaged but you can easily become distracted if you don't have the right information to work with. Issues like an incomplete email, a skipped step or a misleading phone message can mess up your focus as you try to make sense of the situation.

CHAPTER 4

BENEFITS OF BEING FOCUSED

So far it is safe to say that being focused can help yield great benefits not only for the mind and body but the overall life quality of a person. Here is how being focused can help you achieve greater success and control of your life:

Helps take control

When you are focused, you can take control of the things that you are doing. But if you are not focused, that task or thing will end up controlling you. Once you become focused on something and you have channelled all your energy into that particular task, you can handle the task in a better way.

Control will also come easy when you apply all the three types of focus simultaneously into all your tasks. Inner focus will keep you on track and away from distractions while paying attention to others makes you more aware. But it is perhaps outer focus that will be most beneficial in gaining control since it gives you the flexibility to give you a contingency plan if needed.

Yields positive energy

Being focused helps harvest positive energy in the body. It also allows you to get yourself out of a negative spiral and put things into perspective.

When you look at different aspects of daily life, the instinctive reaction is to pay attention to the deficits and focus on what's wrong.

And because attention amplifies everything, focusing on the negative aspects will make everything worse. Instead, it is best to detach from the problem and reinvest focus on how to make the best out of a bad situation.

Everyday obstacles are an unavoidable occurrence, but when you focus on the positive it can help you get through difficult times more steadily.

Perhaps scenarios like this will demand that you bring out your inner focus fully since such situations affects the individual personally. The same can also create chaos in life, so focusing on the positive can help reduce or get rid of this chaos completely.

Enhances problem solving skills

One of the most important benefits of staying focused is that it refines your problem solving skills. If you are not focused, you will never make it through a problem.

The way an individual approaches a problem can vary greatly. For instance, one person may focus more on the on the reason of the problem than the solution, and the other vice versa. The former of these will have *problem-focused thinking* while the latter will engage in *solution-focused thinking*.

Of the two, problem focused thinking will not help solve anything but solution focused thinking can yield the opposite result.

Instills decision making skills

The ability to make decisions is crucial for survival and cannot be executed without focus. Successful decision making is based on the principles of logical and critical thinking which need to be focus based. Whether you are a boss or an employee, whether you are a parent or a student, you need to make several decisions either on daily basis or on occasional basis. None of the decisions can be made until and unless you are completely focused on the issue.

In addition, the issue does not resolve by simply making any decision, but it has to be the right one. Plus making the right decision also involves executing it correctly. The process includes identifying critical decisions and filtering out unimportant ones.

Making the right decision also means you need to focus on getting the right information to make a good decision.

Removes distractions

Success is not something that can be achieved without determination and will power. To have both these attributes, you need to focus on getting rid of distractions.

While it may seem that people who are highly organized and successful are just like everybody, this is not the case. Instead, they have several habits that are associated with the elimination of distractions from their life.

Distractions can take you away from your goals and aims. Even on daily basis, even the most common distraction can make the completion of the task an impossibility. Thus, you need to stay focused because it is only through staying focused that you can succeed in getting rid of distractions.

Once you are able to do that, there is nothing stopping you from achieving your goals or getting your tasks done. At the end of the day, it always comes down to how focused you are on your goal. If you ask any famous and successful person, you would see that focus was a big part of their story. It's because what you constantly focus on will eventually become your reality.

Gets things done

This is probably the one benefit of being focused that we all feel in our daily life. If you stay focused, there is a better chance of you being able to finish something you started or complete something that you are supposed to do. Anyone who is not focused tends to postpone the task to some next day or other time and as a result, the task remains undone. Being focused is a demand of every profession and every field of life. In every single sphere of life, you will need to be focused to get done what needs to get done.

Generates satisfaction

Staying focused also makes you feel content with yourself and everyone else around you. If you are not focused on one thing and your mind is always wandering around, you will have more pressure and stress on your mind and body. This robs you of any peace that you could hope for.

When you're focused, you can just keep one thing in front of your eyes and work on it diligently. Your brain and body will be in sync with what you need to accomplish at that given time.

Builds momentum

Focus increases effectiveness which in turn lets you progress faster with your tasks. The faster you get your scheduled tasks out of the way, the greater your productivity.

Focus based momentum also helps you stay on track and prevents derailing. On the other hand, changing direction deflates momentum and disturbs focus as well. This point can also tie in with multitasking where you may be trying to get too much done at one time, and every task suffers. So to stay in momentum, start a job on time, finish it all the way through and then move on to the next task.

Reduces stress

Staying focused also helps reduce stress as all your concentration will be on the task at hand. A lack of focus, on the other hand, leads to becoming overwhelmed with too much to do and too little time.

Being overwhelmed also impairs your judgement on where to start and that can be stressful too. With focus, clarity becomes improved, allows you to get out of overwhelm which, in turn reduces stress and leads to improved outcomes.

With clarity intact, you can see the progress you are making and will work with focus to achieve your desired results.

Increases engagement

Focus gives direction and purpose to a task. In this sense it engages the interest and effort of the individual. With a clear cut target in sight, you will not be hesitant to put in additional effort, since most people are not afraid of hard work but the possibility of failure.

When goals are not articulated, it becomes hard and even impossible to focus on how to achieve them. So focus oriented direction will pique interest and engagement in all scenarios.

CHAPTER 5

HOW HIGHLY SUCCESSFUL PEOPLE
DEVELOP SELF-DISCIPLINE

What most people have in common with successful people is ambition, but where certain fall short and others excel is in the area of self-discipline.

According to Dennis Prager, "Happiness is dependent on self- discipline." The biggest hurdle in achieving our goals is how easily we let ourselves be distracted by things that do not count as progress towards our achievements.

However, practicing self-discipline is not easy and demands real commitment. In order to develop self-discipline, you must follow certain steps that will help you attain your goals. Here are the top habits of successful people that help that maintain self-discipline which ultimately helps them achieve their goals:

Vision

Highly successful people know exactly where they want to be in life. They know exactly where you want to go. It is impossible to be successful without knowing where you want to be.

In order to be successful, create a vision board. Curate pictures and quotes that motivate you to achieve what you want to and look at it before you start your day. This will help you align your tasks with your goals. In order to visualize, you must have a conscious purposefulness which helps you in clearing up your headspace.

Prioritize

Another thing about self-disciplined people is that they finish their important tasks before they allow themselves any indulgences.

It is very important to prioritize everything so that you face less distraction during your day. Getting important tasks done first relieves the pressure of an undone task and also gives you plenty of time to be productive for the rest of the day.

For instance, if working on your next project will help you be successful in future then it is important you work on it before you let yourself spend time with friends, on your phone etc. As the saying goes, "Being lazy is the best reward for finishing tasks now."

Say no to distractions

The strongest habit of highly successful people is their courage to say no to distractions. Successful people are just as prone to get distracted by social media and hangouts as you but they square up and say no in order to work toward their goals.

This does not mean you can never indulge with social media presence or go out with friends but prioritizing your work is important.

Many people lack the courage to say no to a hang out when they know they should be working. Once you have learned to say you will notice that you are moving towards your goals. It is so easy to get distracted by people who are chilling but "Don't get distracted by people who are not on track."

Handle one task at a time

Highly successful people are realistic with their to-do lists. If you have spent a lot of your days procrastinating then it is impossible to suddenly finish everything in a day. Start by trying to focus on one task at a time instead of overwhelming yourself with the thought of everything that is not finished.

"If the finish line feels too far away, don't look at it." Keep yourself focused on what you have at hand and make sure that you do your best while you are at it.

Divide up goals

Once you have a bigger goal in mind it is important that you divide it in smaller chunks. You need to know all the steps that you must take in order to achieve what you want. Instead of moping around, get realistic. Divide your goal into what needs to be done each day, each week, each month or in six months.

"A goal without plan is just a wish." You cannot expect everything you want to magically appear in front of you. It takes hard work and every successful person in history put that hard work in to turn their dreams into reality.

Rewards and breaks

You cannot stay focused unless you give yourself sufficient breaks during the day. Every business, school or workplace has breaks after a certain period because the body cannot function continuously for so long without resting. So if you want to keep distractions at bay, it is essential to take breaks during the day or working period.

It is important that you acknowledge your hard work because your mind is more likely to stay focused on goals when you give it breaks. Otherwise you will physically and mentally feel overwhelmed and burn yourself out. After each day of doing what you intended to, reward yourself with an hour of social media, dinner with friends or just staying in and chilling on your own. This will also energize you and motivate you to work the next day.

Make sure that you take one day each week where you don't do anything. This is important in order to give you a break before you start working again.

Learn from mistakes

Another thing that highly successful people do is learn from their mistakes instead of quitting. So what if you made a mistake? It only adds to your experience and teaches you about how to maneuver things better.

Every time you make a mistake, remind yourself that it is a blessing. The more mistakes you make the more you take yourself on the right path. Every goal is an accumulation of lessons that you learned from your mistakes along the way.

Rise above feelings

When we know what we need to do our feelings can be contagious and deceptive. We can make ourselves believe that we can take a break after one day of working hard or two days of working hard. Consistency is the key to achievement.

Don't argue with the plan you have made for yourself. It is only habitual to deny hard work because we become accustomed to laziness. If you want to achieve something don't be passive to feelings that lead to destruction of your plan.

You will have plenty of time for laziness, self-pity and fatigue when you are done with your tasks.

Love what you do

It is important that you look at hard work as a positive trait rather than something that strains you. When we force ourselves to work hard it is natural to hate it because we cannot waste time anymore. Successful people love their work and therefore it is easier for them to put in the effort that is needed to achieve their goals.

Whenever you feel distressed because of all that you need to get done, remind yourself why you are doing it in the first place. This will help you develop a positive mindset towards your work.

Manipulate energy

Self-disciplined people do not burn themselves out. Instead, they devote their effort to tasks that need energy. Sometimes people make the mistake of building up all their energy for a task that does not need as much energy and later they feel tired or fatigued because they used it all up.

In order to achieve your goals, know what demands your active motivation and what you can do without using effort. This is a difficult task for those who are starting from zero therefore start by taking up one task and perfecting it until it becomes habit.

Then add another and slowly build up to it. "Relax but don't get too comfortable." Your mind will fool you into believing that you have done a lot when you achieve one goal but it is not always true.

In a nutshell, you can keep reading tips on self-discipline but the real effort is to apply them in real life. Instead of looking around for more tips, start practicing them now.

As perhaps one of his most famous quotes, Steve Jobs said, "If today were the last day of your life, would you want to do what you are about to do?"

Always look ahead in future. If you dream of success then it is time to push away all your distractions and start working on your goals.

CHAPTER 6

STRATEGIES TO BUILDING
UNBREAKABLE FOCUS

Whether you are a student, a parent or a worker, you are aware of the importance of focus for everything that you do in your life. Whether there is a short term plan to follow, or a long term goal neither can be accomplished without focus.

There are a few strategies that you can use to build unbreakable focus. Once you succeed in making these strategies a part of your life, you will be much more in touch with yourself and you will experience a self of accomplishment that nothing else can give you.

Train your brain

This is the most essential part of the focus building process. Your brain controls everything that goes on in your body. Whether it is something you think or something you see or it is something that you feel, everything is controlled by your brain. This is why you need to have extensive control over your brain and you need to train it to stay focused.

Make a habit of repeating the task at hand, to yourself again and again. Prepare yourself mentally for what you are about to do. Before you do anything, sit in a quiet place and let it sink into your brain that you are going to spend the next few hours on a specific task. This is a mind strengthening exercise that you need to do to keep focused. If you train your brain well enough, it will not be side tracked by any distractions after that.

Plan it all out

Before you start anything, you need to plan it all out. This does not only apply to everyday tasks but it also applies to long term tasks. For example, businesses that tend to have business plan for a year or a semester have a better chance of increasing sales and making a mark. When you plan something, you lay all the tasks out in front of you.

This makes it easier for you to determine which things require your utmost attention. Using this plan, you can also schedule the time for the completion of your task and you can divide every task of yours into time intervals.

When you know that you have to finish a particular task in a given time frame, you will be able to maintain your focus better.

Rest for a while

The human body is not made for functioning constantly, which is why the concept of sleep is present in the body. No matter how much work needs to be done, you need to rest for a while. Take a half an hour break after every 4 or 5 hours that you work. This would help to freshen up your brain and it will also give you time to relax. During this time, you can clear your brain and simply give time to yourself.

By resting or taking breaks, you can quickly build up focus. This strategy has proven to be successful even by scientific methods.

Workplaces have a lunch break and other breaks during the day so that employees can stay productive for the whole day. This is particularly important if you are doing an extensive activity. It becomes harder to focus so you need to give your brain and body a break. In these few minutes or half an hour, do what soothes your body. Listen to calming music or simply go for a walk in some calm neighbourhood.

Work with music

This strategy may not work with everyone but it has shown to be successful in most cases. Listening to music is something most people enjoy. You could try by playing your favourite music in the background while you work. It is better if the song is not too loud because that can cause distraction.

The music must not be too loud to distract you from the work that you are doing. However, people who are prone to dancing around with their favourite music on may not benefit from this strategy as much.

Practice mindfulness

Using mindfulness to build focus is probably one of the best techniques. The key step involved is to sit in a quiet place and take a deep breathe in. After that, you are required to hold your breath for a few seconds and then exhale. It is during this pause that you need to bring your mind back to the thing that it needs to be on.

Your mind tends to drift away every once in a while because the lifespan of human concentration is merely 8 seconds. It is due to this reason that you need to make this exercise a habit so that you can benefit from it. It also serves as a reliever of stress and can rid the body of any negative energy. Once you harbour positive energy in the body and you shift your brain's function to one task, your focus will automatically improve.

Since we are all creatures of habit, integrating the right habits into your workday will help immensely. Once something becomes a habit, it also becomes easy. If focusing becomes a habit, it will come to you naturally and will let you have multiple benefits on a daily basis.

Limit phone usage

A major distraction for many people is cell phone usage and portable technology. It can easily distract you from the task that you are supposed to do.

Most students can relate to situations where they have assignments or pending projects but instead, they are busy on their cell phones.

So while you are working, make sure that you put your phone away to avoid being distracted by incoming calls or messages. If you work on your phone, install an app which lets you block notifications from social media sites.

In instances where you do not have any specific work to do on the phone, there can still be an inclination to use it for social media. This is another thing that can distract you from your task and ultimately your goals.

Set a time for using your phone. Sometime in the evening or after dinner is a good timeslot for this type of activity. Most people are done with their day's work by dinner time and may use their phone as much as they want.

Give constant reminders

Another way to get rid of distractions is to constantly remind yourself about your goals and aims that you hope to accomplish. Once you do that, you will be inclined towards doing what you actually need to do instead of wasting your time on unnecessary things.

Any business person or individual hoping to make a mark constantly reminds himself of the goal he is hoping to achieve. A daily reminder first thing in the morning is a good place to start.

Plan your day

Another way to keep distractions away is to plan your day beforehand. When you go to bed, make a habit to make a little plan for the next day in your mind. Keep the unnecessary things out of it and make sure that you sort out the things according to the amount of time you have on your hands and the task that need to be done first.

When you do so, your brain will slowly be trained to only pay attention to the tasks that you have planned for that day. It is also useful to have a planner or a diary that you can keep with you. People who have a diary are more organized and they tend to get more work done on time.

When you make this a habit, you will be able to stick to your schedule. It is the hardest to not deviate from the plan but with practice, it can become second nature. This habit can lead to success and your brain will automatically cancel out any task it finds unnecessary that is, any task not mentioned in the plan.

Having positive energy is very important as it energizes the body for functioning in the best way possible.

CHAPTER 7

WHY SHOULD YOU FOCUS
ON ONE THING AT A TIME

Multitasking is basically trying to split focus and divide your attention to getting multiple projects done at a time. While many believe that this practice actually gets more done, that may not always be the case. Instead, while trying to increase the quantity of jobs being performed, you may well be compromising the quality of every one of them.

The result is hurting your own productivity while shifting focus from one task to the other without being fully attentive to any single one. Instead, here is a look at why you should only focus on one thing at a time.

It gets things done

The best part about doing one thing at a time is that it gets things done. When you focus all your attention and your energy to one thing, you ensure that the particular task will get done and it will be done on time. For you to accomplish any task, you need to have excessive focus. The thing about focus is that it gets diverted easily if there are more things on your mind.

When you are doing one thing at a time, your focus is only on that one task and it gets done in a timely manner. On the contrary, if you try to do three things at the same time, then your focus will be divided between them and you will not be able to do any single one of them.

It leaves less room for error

Everyone who does more than one thing at a single time knows that there is a much greater chance of error when you are doing more things at one time. On the other hand, when you give your undivided attention on one thing only, you can do it with much more accuracy. In fact, multitasking is actually switching between tasks and when it boils down to concentration and productivity, the brain only has a limited amount.

A common example is people using their cell phones while driving. Since you are not focusing on one thing only, there is a huge margin for error. Even in less impacting issues such as texting, this phenomenon can be seen. If you text four or five people at the same time, there is a likelihood that you will end up sending the wrong thing to the wrong person. It is due to this reason that you need to keep your focus on one thing only.

Accomplishment of tasks should not be your only goal. Your goal should be to do the task in the best way possible with minimum error. To make this possible, it is essential to stay focused on one thing at a single time and not have a lot of different things to do at the same time.

Higher success rate

If you focus on one thing at a time, you end up having a better chance of succeeding at something. This is not only applicable in the case of businesses or entrepreneurs but also in any everyday situation. People who try to do only one thing at a time are more likely to be attentive as well than those who try to do everything at the same time.

In the same way, the probability of being successful is higher if you focus on one thing at a time. Businesses tend to focus on one thing for the time being, such as making their marketing more efficient or increasing employee productivity instead of trying to do all of these things at once. It is not possible to juggle so many things at once so the better approach is to take one step at a time.

It does not deplete energy

If you have a habit of doing many things at one time, you will always be tired and will suffer from a lack of energy. This is why it is better to focus on one thing instead of trying to go for three or four things.

The human brain may be like a machine when it comes to its functionality but it has the human character of tiredness.

It gets tired after long hours of activity or after doing many things at the same time. When you try to do a lot of things at the same time, you are putting a lot of strain on the brain. As a result of this, the energy reserves of the body are exploited which leads to a decrease in the energy levels of the body.

You might feel that you are capable of doing many things at the same time but the truth is that the internal functioning of your body is not entirely invisible to you. So, you cannot really know how an activity is harming the inside of your body.

If you focus on one thing at a time, you can direct your brain to do the same thing for a precise period of time. When your brain only has to accomplish one task at a time, it can function more effectively. However, if you are trying to cook, clean and write an essay at the same time, the brain and body are going to have a hard time trying to keep up with the levels of your activity.

If your work involves physical work, it can also tire out your body and when the body is not active, there is no way you can focus on a task to make it more successful. When your glucose levels run out, your body function also decreases.

It keeps distractions away

Another benefit of doing one thing at a time is that it keeps distractions at bay. When you try to do more than one task at a time, you will find your brain wandering off to the other task that needs to be done. Using the example mentioned above, if you are trying to cook but your brain is constantly focused on the content you need for your essay, it is not unlikely that you will be successful in any of your tasks.

You may be able to cook and finish your essay but the essay is not going to be the best you have ever written and the cooking is not going to be satisfactory. When you focus all your attention and concentration onto one thing, you can easily accomplish your task as your brain is only thinking of the current task at hand.

It lets you enjoy work

Let's admit it. If you are trying to juggle too many things at the same time, you will not be able to enjoy any of it. Just imagine writing emails while having dinner. There is no way you are going to enjoy your dinner due to the distraction and it is also probable that you will end up making mistakes in your emails.

Similarly, at work or during studying, if you do not focus on one thing at a time, you will not be able to enjoy it. Most people do not enjoy their work because they are trying to manage a whole lot of tasks at once. When you start doing one thing at a time, you will find the process more enjoyable and easier to accomplish.

Conclusively, multitasking can prove to be pretty unproductive as lower quality work is produced, more mistakes are made and both time and effort get wasted.

CHAPTER 8

ONLINE TOOLS FOR LASER FOCUS

The hardest thing for most people is to live in the present moment. It has become difficult to stay focused on one task with so many distractions around us. But this type of lifestyle also affects our efficiency at the workplace as our mind wanders and we struggle to finish our tasks on time.

However, while the internet has provided us with multiple distractions in form of social media it has also generated tools which can be helpful in organizing time and finishing tasks on time. Here is a list of some applications that will help you regain your laser focus and control your time instead of letting internet distractions control it:

1. StayFocused

StayFocused is an extension that works on Chrome. There are many ad blockers or website blockers that can be added to Chrome. However, this one is designed to help you get work done instead of spending hours on Twitter or Facebook. You can also set break times which means you can set time where you will be allowed to enter websites but as soon as your break time is over you will not be allowed to enter them again.

The "Nuclear Option" is for those who absolutely cannot resist their distractions. This will not let you enter any of the websites that keep you from working and it cannot be deactivated until after the provided time period.

2. Freedom

This is an application for web, pc, iOS and Mac that can be installed to block out websites that distract you so you can pay attention to what needs to be done. Making to-do lists is fun but getting everything done on your to-do list is a challenge when you have a habit of spending hours scrolling through your favorite social media.

Freedom lets you manage schedules so you can block certain websites for a certain time period. For instance, if you spend hours scrolling through Facebook, you can add it on Freedom app to block it from 9:00 AM to 2:00 PM while you finish your work. Freedom will not let you enter the land of distraction within the scheduled time.

It also has a "Locked Mode" which can be turned on to prevent from breaking the given schedule and giving in to your craving for social media. When you have a habit of procrastination, it is impossible to avoid going back to that lifestyle but with locked mode you can easily avoid it.

3. FocusWriter

This application is for those whose work requires a lot of writing. However, many writers struggle with focusing on their writing while working on their laptops. If you also struggle with staying focused on your work then this is a great website which pops-up a plain grey background to write on and everything else is blocked away including timer and date until your scheduled time is over.

FocusWriter also includes features like word count and spell-check which are crucial to writing jobs and assignments. It also has certain other features like setting a writing goal which will bring gratification once you have achieved your goal. Besides that the typewriting sounds with each key make it interesting to work with FocusWriter.

4. Concentrate

This application is designed to manage different types of tasks. Sometimes people can start their day really motivated to get everything done but after one task they tend to get distracted before they can start the next task. Concentrate will block out the email client and browser to keep you away from Buzzfeed,

YouTube, Twitter etc. while you are writing. Launch applications feature allows you to access only the applications that are needed for tasks in hand.

The "Speak a Message" feature allows you to record a message that will play on set time and motivate you to concentrate on your work. This Mac application is designed to help you stick to your schedule for the day until you have finished everything.

5. Be Focused

Be Focused application uses Pomodro technique because it has been proven that people tend to focus on their tasks better if they take breaks in between. Many people struggle to take a break from fear of losing attention but they end up losing focus with time. Be Focused will give you short breaks after 25 minutes of working and longer intervals before you switch from one task to another.

You can create a list of tasks and track your progress as you move along. This iOS application is perfect if you don't want to lose enthusiasm as you progress. You will get time to rejuvenate your headspace and be ready to take up the next task efficiently.

6. Forest

If you feel like your phone is chained to your hands and keep you from working then Forest app will help you leave it be while you finish your work. This is an interesting application that allows you to grow a forest. Whenever you activate it, you plant a tree and the tree will die if you interrupt or deactivate.

Forest application has partnered with Trees for the Future and every tree you make is actually being planted in the world. This means that each tree you plant will earn you virtual coins which will be spent on plantation of trees.

7. Hold

Hold is an application that is specially designed for students and keeps an eye on their activity. If you struggle with studying or finish your papers because you cannot resist Instagram feed and Facebook comments then this application is for you. For every 20 minutes that you spend away from your phone, you earn a point.

When you have earned fifteen points you get a reward in shape of raffle tickets or coffee from 7-eleven. Many students who have used this application testified that their grades improved by using the Hold app.

8. Noisli

Some people tend to focus better on their application when they are surrounded by an ideal ambience. Noisli provides ambient noises like seaside, bonfire crackles, fan etc. so you can customize a combination of your favorite sounds so you can have the perfect atmosphere to work in.

Noisli is therefore an application for those who want to work in a particular environment which will help them stay focused on the task. Noisli also has another feature inspired by Pomodro techniques which helps you divide your tasks and Chromotherapy inspired feature lets you choose a certain background color while you work.

9. Balanced

Balanced is an application that helps you build your focus by creating a balance in your life. It is important that you maintain a healthy lifestyle that consists of reading, meditation, workout, walking etc. Balanced tracks your time spent on doing things that you wish you did more.

Some people struggle with reading books while other cannot stay focused on yoga. Balanced will keep you motivated to include these tasks in your daily life and stay focused on them.

10. Hocus Focus

Hocus Focus is another application made to improve your productivity by making your browser tab clutter-free. It is no secret that we tend to focus better when we have a cleaner environment. The same is true about working on your PC.

Hocus Pocus will close any website that you are not actively using. For instance if you have distracting applications like Twitter, Buzzfeed, Facebook etc. open in the background then they will shut off while you start working. A research shows that it takes 23 minutes for an average human brain to refocus and a distracting application can make it even harder.

Printed by Libri Plureos GmbH in Hamburg, Germany